About the Book

Possum Baby was afraid. Inside his mother's pouch he had felt snug and secure, surrounded by his nine brothers and sisters. Now he shivered. The cold wind swept across him and an owl hooted far off in the night.

But soon a fierce animal came leaping toward him and Possum Baby discovered his own natural way of defending himself—without fighting back!

Berniece Freschet and Jim Arnosky, who joined talents in their previous book, PORCUPINE BABY, once again create a lively tale of animal life and growing up in the forest.

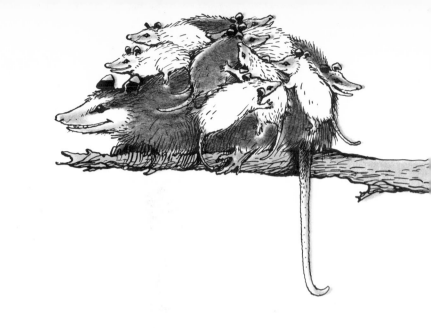

G. P. Putnam's Sons · New York

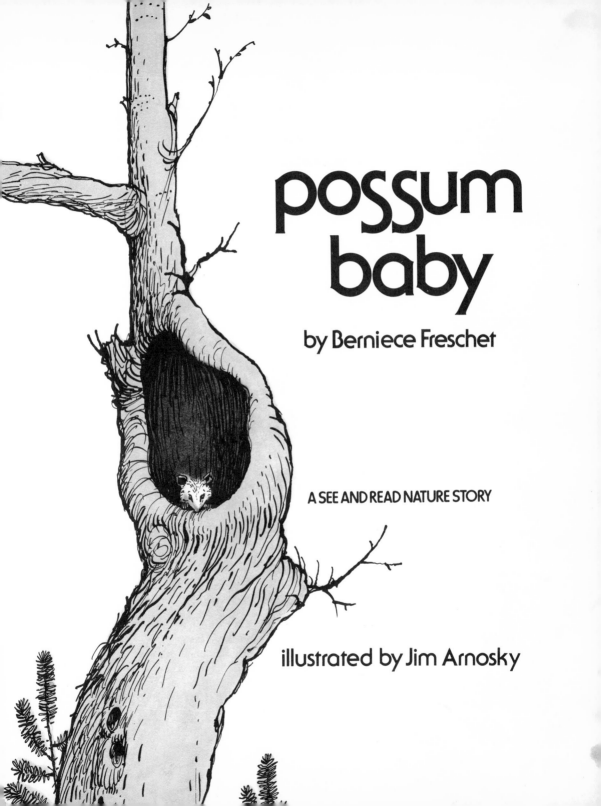

possum baby

by Berniece Freschet

A SEE AND READ NATURE STORY

illustrated by Jim Arnosky

For Rachel, next door

Text copyright © 1978 by Berniece Freschet
Illustrations copyright © 1978 by Jim Arnosky
All rights reserved. Published simultaneously
in Canada by Longman Canada Limited, Toronto.
Printed in the United States of America
06209

Library of Congress Cataloging in Publication Data
Freschet, Berniece.
Possum baby.

(A See and read nature story)
SUMMARY: Presents the life of a baby possum from his
birth into his mother's pouch to his first experience
"playing possum", after which he is on his own.
1.   Virginia opossum—Juvenile literature.
2.   Animals, Infancy of—Juvenile literature.
[1.   Opossums.   2.   Animals—Infancy]
I.   Arnosky, Jim.   II.   Title.
QL737.M34F73   599'.2   77-21000
ISBN 0-399-61105-3 lib. bdg.

Contents

OUT OF THE POUCH

Possum Baby was warm and safe
inside his mother's pouch.
Close about him pressed
nine other little possums.
They had been in the pouch
since they were born,
over two months ago.

When he was first born
Possum Baby was no
bigger than a bee.

His skin was pink.
He had no hair.
His eyes were shut tight,
and he could not hear.

But he had crawled up his mother's fur,

paw over paw,

and into her pouch

all by himself.

WALLABY

Animals with pouches
are called marsupials.

KOALAS

HONEY POSSUM

In Australia many animals
have pouches, but the possum
is the only marsupial
in North America.

As soon as the little possums
were inside their mother's pouch,
they each took hold of a nipple
and began to nurse.
Possum Baby and his brothers
and sisters stayed inside the pouch
nursing and growing until today.
But now they had grown
too big for the pouch.

They wanted out.
And one by one,
out they came—
. . . all except Possum Baby.
Nine little possums crawled
up on their mother's back,
holding tight to her fur.

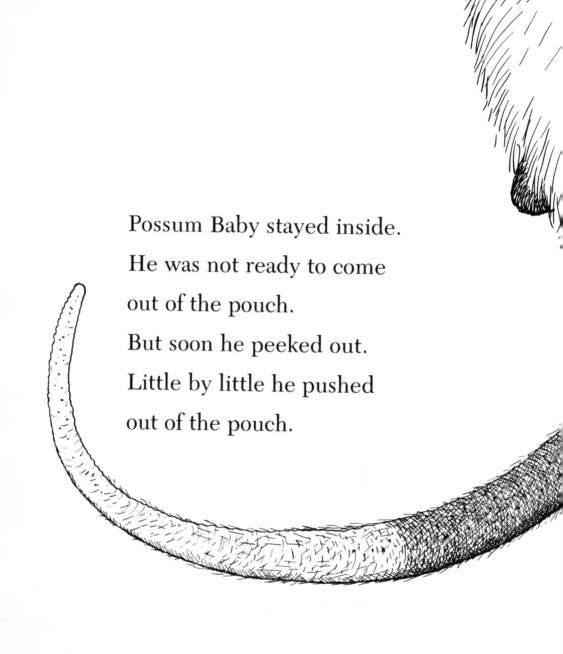

Possum Baby stayed inside.
He was not ready to come
out of the pouch.
But soon he peeked out.
Little by little he pushed
out of the pouch.

Now Possum Baby was about
as big as a mouse.
His black eyes were open.
Soft gray fur covered his body.
Slowly he crawled up
on his mother's back,
his front paws clutching her fur.

Since he was the last one out,
Possum Baby was the last in line.
He held tight to his mother's tail.
It felt strange
outside the pouch
with no warm bodies
close about him.

Here there was only
empty space—
and it was cold.
A wind ruffled his fur.
Possum Baby began to shiver.
He heard an owl hoot
and a dog bark.
What was that?

15

Did the little possum sense
that they were his enemies?
Possum Baby was afraid.
His whole body shook.
A red squirrel ran over
a branch above him.
Leaves brushed against his body.

His heart beat faster.

Quickly Possum Baby crawled

down his mother's side

and pushed back inside the pouch.

Here, inside the pouch,

it was snug, and warm,

. . . and he was *safe*.

AT THE STREAM

Mother Possum poked
her head out of the den.
The den was a hole
in an old hickory tree.
She was hungry.
She climbed out of the hole
and down the tree.

On her back rode

the ten little possums.

Possum Baby was the last in line.

He held tight

to his mother's tail.

Mother Possum took the path
that led to the stream.

It was night but that didn't
bother Mother Possum.
She liked to hunt at night.

Her black eyes could see
well in the darkness.
On her way she stopped often
to turn over rocks and eat
the fat grubs that she found there.

They came to a blackberry bush.
She stopped to eat the berries.
All the little possums got down
to eat the sweet fruit—

—all except for Possum Baby.
He stayed where he was,
holding tight to his mother's tail.

In a little while
the possum family moved on.
They came to the stream.
The water sparkled
in the moonlight.

Mother Possum stopped
beside the stream.
Her feet made tiny
star-tracks in the mud.

The stars were from her five
long toes on each of her paws.
Her long toes helped her
to climb trees.
Mother Possum dipped
her quick fingers into the water.
She pulled out a crayfish.

She cracked the shell
with her sharp teeth.
All the little possums
began to poke their noses
into bushes and under rocks.
They were learning to look
for their own food,
—all except for Possum Baby.
He stayed where he was
on top of his mother's back.

The possums ate almost anything,

ants and earthworms,

fruits and berries,

bulbs and mushrooms,

frogs, and mice, and turtle eggs,

and even little green snakes
when they could catch them.

Finally Possum Baby got tired
of sitting all alone
on his mother's back.
And he was getting hungry.
He came down to see
what the others were doing.
He looked for something to eat.

Under an old tree stump
he found some beetle grubs.
They tasted good.
He heard an owl hoot—
. . . and a dog bark.
There were those *noises* again.
Possum Baby was afraid.

He began to shake
but this time he didn't run
back to his mother's pouch.
He stayed and ate the good-tasting
fat grubs he had found.
Suddenly, a big bullfrog
plopped into the water.
Right in front of Possum Baby's nose

SPLASH

The sudden noise frightened
all the little possums.
They ran to their mother.
And this time, when they
rode back to their den,
Possum Baby was not
the last in line.
This time Possum Baby
rode up front,
holding tight to his mother's ear.

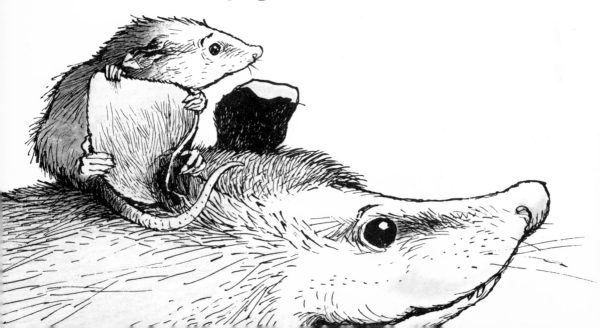

PLAYING POSSUM

The little possums were growing.

They were four months old

and too big now for all of them

to ride on their mother's back.

It was time for them

to be off on their own.

Six of the little possums had
already wandered off by themselves.
But Possum Baby still did not
stray too far from his mother's side.

Possum Baby had grown to look
almost exactly like his mother.
He had the same white, pointed face,

and big black button eyes.
He had the same wide
grinning mouth and sharp teeth.

And he had the long, hairless tail
and velvet-soft ears.
But his fur was darker than his mother's.
It was almost the color of black soot.
Tonight the possums
had found a persimmon tree.

They sat together in the branches,

eating the sweet fruit,

persimmon juice running

down their chins.

When he was done

Possum Baby washed himself all over.

He liked to be clean.

Possum Baby started down the tree.

He wrapped his tail around a branch.

His tail was so strong that he could

hang from the branch, upside down,

just like a monkey.

Tonight the mother possum
did not stop at the stream,
as she often did.
Tonight she found a rocky place
and led her family
from rock to rock,
across to the other side.

Tiny star tracks
covered the muddy banks.
It was a warm summer night
and mother possum knew
of a cornfield not far away.
The ears of yellow corn
should be ripe by now.

In the distance a dog barked.

Possum Baby wasn't quite as afraid.

Soon they were at the farmer's field.

The corn was tall and ripe.

All the little possums ate and ate.

They ate until their stomachs

were fat and full of the

sweet yellow corn.

Possum Baby heard the dog bark,
only now the bark sounded louder.
He heard more barking.
It *was* louder—and *closer*.
Possum Baby was afraid.
All the little possums ran—
one went one way,
and another went another way.
Suddenly, a great animal
ran out of the cornfield.

It was coming straight
for Possum Baby.
It was a fierce-looking animal
—barking and growling!

It snarled, showing it's sharp teeth.

Then the fierce animal jumped right
on top of Possum Baby!
Possum Baby was so afraid
that he fell over on his side.
The little possum's eyes closed
—his tongue hung out
—he lay there, not moving.

Possum Baby looked as if

he were dead!

The dog sniffed at the possum.

Then he pushed him with his nose.

Possum Baby was still—there was

not even a twitch of his tail.

Maybe the little possum was dead.

The dog didn't seem to know what to do.

He pushed at the possum a few more times.

But soon he gave up and turned away.

For a while Possum Baby
lay very still.
Then his ears twitched
and his body shook.
He opened his eyes
and got to his feet.
He looked around.

44

The dog was gone.

There would be many other times

when Possum Baby would be so afraid

that he'd fall down and "play possum."

But never again would he be

quite as afraid.

Possum Baby looked for his mother
and the other little possums.
But they were gone.
He was all alone.

The moon was big and bright.

Possum Baby walked down the path.

From now on he would

take care of himself.

About the Author

Berniece Freschet was educated in her native Montana, first in Miles City and then in Missoula, where she attended the University of Montana.

She now lives in Yorktown Heights, New York, with her husband and five children.

In 1974 Mrs. Freschet won both the Irma Simonton Black Award and the New York Academy of Sciences Children's Book Award. Mrs. Freschet's previous books for Putnam's are PORCUPINE BABY, BIOGRAPHY OF A BUZZARD and WUFU: THE STORY OF THE LITTLE BROWN BAT.

About the Artist

Jim Arnosky is a self-taught artist who lives with his wife and two daughters in Ryegate, Vermont.

Jim's activities vary with the seasons. He fishes, hikes, gardens, and bird- and animal-watches, and, of course, draws all year round.

He is the author/illustrator of I WAS BORN IN A TREE AND RAISED BY BEES and he is the illustrator of POR-CUPINE BABY, a companion volume to POSSUM BABY.